# SPEAK IT

your love &
support! I truly
thank God for

# TILL

you!

# I SEE IT

Peace & Blessings!

*Rod Shipp*

# ROD SHIPP

ISBN 978-1-312-46736-1

Imprint: Lulu.com

This book is dedicated to my grandmothers Helen Arnett and Erma Bowles. They ALWAYS spoke life into me no matter what my circumstances looked like nor what anyone said about me. In their mind, I was on my way to success and there was no other option. My love for these two ladies is stronger than any force on this planet.

# __Preface__

I am, and have been, a firm believer that there is power in the tongue. I truly think that a great majority of what we experience in life is a direct result of what we say, and in most cases, what we don't say. As I mentioned in my last book, "Current Mood: Staying Ready To Succeed", we are destined to experience 'something'. Regardless of how you feel about it, life HAS to present a good or bad scenario. Most of the time, we just go with the flow and allow life to happen as it may. What if you could control or create the flow? What if 'life' is looking to you for instructions on what to do next, but since you didn't provide anything, life has to produce the bare minimum because 'something' has to happen? What if things could shift and become better for you simply by saying the right things? Well, let's start here. The bible says in Genesis 1:1 that in the beginning God created the heavens and the earth. It mentioned a couple verses later that God _said_, "let there be light" and there was light. He continued to say what He wanted and then it was. Now, let's move down to verse 26 where He says, "Let us make mankind in our image and in our likeness." If we have been created with the very likeness of the Creator, meaning having the same ability to speak the things that we want or need, then what's stopping us from doing so? I'll tell you what's stopping us. We simply lack the habit and belief in doing it. This book has been designed and created to form in you the habit of speaking life into your environment. You will embark on a journey of intentionally creating your atmosphere and the need for the life you desire. Results are not typical. There must be a strong belief built towards what you say and do. You have to understand that nothing in life is easy. It will take determination and focus behind the intention in which you will act upon. Remember to follow the steps of this guide daily for the next year and be extremely honest with yourself while completing the exercises. Most importantly, believe in the change that is going to take place as you create the habit of speaking positive and eradicating the negative. I believe that you will be exceedingly great with peace and prosperity to follow you for the rest of your life. I speak good vibes over you and may the right people stay beside you in your corner. May the positive energy that is created in you attract even more positive energy from your surroundings. You are beyond blessed and amazing. Life is only going up from here. I pray that you enjoy the book and find great results from the content.

Peace and Blessings!

Rod Shipp

# Instructions

1. At the beginning of each week, write the dates for that week in the top blank.

2. Each morning, Monday through Saturday, speak the affirmations word for word, while facing yourself in the mirror. Feel free at any time during the week to change up a few words, such as your initial greeting.

3. On Sunday, it is IMPERATIVE that you find 20 minutes minimum to sit in a comfortable, quiet place and mentally create what you want to see for your life at that moment. Don't think too far into the future. Let's focus on the next 6 to 8 months. See yourself doing the things that you want to do or life simply as you would like it to look. Listen to the sound of the ocean or rain if you need to. I've noticed that classical music helps as well.

4. Complete the recap and activities page after each week's affirmations as a guide to refer back and monitor the results. If possible, do

this on Sunday's after your reflection is completed.

5. Lastly, have fun! This is not only designed to create a habit of positive speaking to yourself, but also a chance for you to really connect with yourself. The first good thing you will hear every day will come directly from yourself. Now that's how you get a day started.

# Week 1: _____

The purpose of this week is very critical. One of the biggest reasons why many people don't think about speaking positive things into their life is because of habit. This week, we will set the tone and create a shift in the atmosphere around us as we speak positive words. Are you ready? Smile. Let's go!

"Good morning (say your name). Today was created with you in mind. Today will be a great day as all of the days moving forward will be. No matter what happens I will continue to smile. My heart has joy. Peaceful people will encounter me today. I love life. I am a blessing to those around me. Today is better than yesterday because yesterday is gone and I am still here. Smile (say your name) because you are winning!"

# Week 1 Recap and Activity

How comfortable were you at the start of the week saying the affirmation? (Rate 1-10 with 10 as the most comfortable) _____

Using the same scale, how did you feel by the end of the week? _____

What was your reflection focused on and why is that important to you?

_____

_____

_____

_____

_____

What would you like to see change in your life in the next 3 months?

_____

_____

_____

_____

_____

# Week 2: _____

The ability to believe what you say when speaking affirmations increases the moment you make it a habit. Every day will not be easy and there will be times when you absolutely don't feel like doing it. Do it anyway. Negative energy has been a factor in everyone's lives and the forces that come with that energy do not want to see you advance. Fight against it and stay on course. We are fighting this battle together!

"Good morning (say your name). I want to tell you how great you are. Your peace changes the course of a day. Your smile illuminates a room. Nothing can defeat you. You are stronger than anything negative. You will attract the attention of positive people. God will lead you in the way you should go. You got this. Even you can't stop you. Your positive vibrations are strong! The day is yours!"

# Week 2 Recap and Activity

If you could change anything negative about yourself and make it positive, what would it be and how would you make it positive?

_____

_____

_____

_____

How can you becoming more positive affect the closest people to you?

_____

_____

_____

_____

How difficult is it for you to visualize the way you want life to be during the reflection process? (Rate 1-10 with 10 being the most difficult) _____

Why did you choose this rating?

_____

_____

# Week 3: _____

It's very important to say the things you don't see right now as if they already exist. Don't worry about what's not visible at the moment. Keep speaking it until you see it come to fruition. Doesn't matter if you are sick, speak healing. Don't worry about the bank account says, speak increase.

"(Say your name), you are amazing. Today, you woke up healed and whole. You are well off financially and are a lender and not the borrower. The people in your life are blessed because they have you. The journey that you are on will create a life of peace for you. Everything that you desire will be yours. That (say **house, car, or position at work**; whichever you want most) will be yours. It's coming (say your name). Oh it's coming!"

# Week 3 Recap and Activity

What's one thing you desire the most right now, such as a car, house, or a certain job?

_____

_____

What steps are you currently taking to obtain that desire?

_____

_____

_____

_____

How do you feel about blessing others and helping them towards their goals?

_____

_____

_____

How did you feel about your reflection time today and what did you visualize?

_____

_____

# Week 4: _____

      One thing that I've learned over the years is that there is no greater enemy than the one I create within me. Most of the time, we miss out on opportunities not from lack of knowledge or resources, but simply from verbal assassination. This week, we will change that.

"Good morning (say beautiful or handsome). Today was masterfully made with you (point to yourself in the mirror) in mind. I am not only destined for greatness, but I will leave an imprint on someone's heart. People will look to me for inspiration and many will find it. There may be times when the enemy tries to strike, but I will not assist in that attempt. I AM MY BEST SUPPORTER! I believe in the power in me given by my Creator! No matter what, I will win."

# Week 4 Recap and Activity

Explain the feeling you get when you see yourself
winning in your visions and what does that look like?

_____

_____

_____

_____

Name one thing that you've learned about yourself in
these last 4 weeks that you believe was not there
before and why do you think it's there now?

_____

_____

_____

_____

What's the main obstacle you must conquer to fully
become your best supporter?

_____

_____

_____

_____

_____

# Week 5: _____

For years, I believe that I was held back because I blamed myself for decisions I'd made or things that I failed to correct. Forgiveness is not something we must give to those who hurt us. It is also an act that we must provide for ourselves. And this week we will.

"Mr./Ms./Mrs. (say your name), hello. For a long time you have dealt with certain things that were out of your control. There were times when you made a decision that was not the best. But both of those times are dead and gone and today is what we have. Tomorrow doesn't exist so right now is what's important. I forgive you (point to yourself) for the things of the past that may have affected you later. You are greater now than ever before. And that my friend is ALL that matters. Be great today."

# Week 5 Recap and Activity

Let's clear the air. What is the one thing that has held you back mentally for way too long and why?

_____

_____

_____

_____

What are a couple of steps you can take to move forward and grow from that situation?

_____

_____

_____

Self-love is imperative for one to have in order to grow in life. Thinking about this week's affirmation, how important is maintaining forgiveness for yourself from here on out and why?

_____

_____

_____

_____

# Week 6: _____

Words have so much power. There are certain words that I believe everyone must hear from time to time that could generate more confidence and inner peace. This week we will focus on saying some impactful words to get your spirit moving.

"Great morning (sir/ma'am). Today is a new day filled with many victories. I am a victor. I am an important piece to any puzzle. My mind is focused and sharp. I will not be easily distracted. My goals for today will be met and I will have joy completing them. I am the cream of the crop in my (business/company). I will strive to continue being the best. Even during challenges, I will not be frustrated. I will simply get the job done. This is what I do. Let's win big today (say your name)!"

# Week 6 Recap and Activity

How do you feel this week's affirmation contributed to the successes of your week?

_____

_____

_____

What challenge did you experience this week and what positive way did you choose to handle it?

_____

_____

_____

_____

Take a second and write down as many positive words you could use when describing yourself. (i.e. smart, magnificent, motivated, etc).

_____

_____

_____

_____

_____

# Week 7: _____

Titles have a way of increasing ones confidence. Many times we would see a person light up from being called certain titles. This week let's use catch words and titles to increase our positive vibrations. You never know. You may just attract a new position in your life.

"Good morning boss. I am the master of my fate. I am the general of my internal army. I will continue to fight for my dreams and nothing will stand in my way. I am a natural born leader created by God Himself. Per His design, I was born to be a conqueror. I do not lose, but I learn from my mistakes. I am the CEO of (say your full name) Enterprises. Today is the day that I begin my quest to the top of Victory mountain. And I will do this with one successful step at a time."

# Week 7 Recap and Activity

Why do you think titles may be important for enhancing your confidence?

_____

_____

_____

What lessons have you learned from losses you've experienced?

_____

_____

_____

What are a few titles you can call yourself that are valid now or you would love to hear being called about you in the future?

_____

_____

What does it mean to be the CEO of your life?

_____

_____

_____

# Week 8: _____

Compliments have a way of moving butterflies around in a person's heart. The scary truth is many people go weeks, months, and sometimes years before hearing heartfelt compliments about them. This week we will be responsible for creating that joy for ourselves.

"(Say your name), I just want to start the day by saying I love you. I admire the pride that you take in your personal growth. I see you as an amazing individual filled with great energy always ready to conquer the day. You are thoughtful. You are patient. You are caring. And you are remarkable. God really took His time when He made you. And it shows. Today, you will be brilliant. Go get it done (Mr./Ms./Mrs.) (say your last name)!"

# Week 8 Recap and Activity

What attributes do you love about yourself?

_____

_____

_____

_____

What are some things that you could do to show more love to yourself?

_____

_____

_____

_____

_____

How important do you think it is to show yourself more love than anyone else could show you and why?

_____

_____

_____

_____

_____

# Week 9: _____

Recognizing the need to have joy in life is a task that many simply ignore. Life is supposed to be a gift. If that's the case then there should be an overwhelming feeling of happiness as it relates to living. Let's be intentional this week in inviting joy into our lives.

"Hey (say your name). First off, great morning to you. I know that life is a gift. I know that I deserve peace and joy. I know that today is a blessing. I am loved and I am important to those around me. Simply meeting me gives one a piece of happiness. My joy comes from God. He gave me today and I will let no one take the joy that God brings away from me. I own my smile. I own my peace. Today I have complete joy!"

# Week 9 Recap and Activity

Name five things in life that give you joy.

_____

_____

_____

_____

In what way could you possibly bring more joy into your life? I want you to take a second and think about how you can change some things that debilitate your joy and what you can replace them with.

_____

_____

_____

_____

_____

Why is it important for you to have joy and are you committed to seeking it more for your life?

_____

_____

_____

# Week 10: _____

    Being intelligent and making wise decisions may seem practical to many. It's easy to say that someone should have made a better choice at something. Truth is, as humans, most of the decisions and choices we make are not led by intellect, but by the emotion of the moment. This week, we will strategically place our minds in position to bypass the "moments" and speak life simply on making better instinctive choices.

    "(Say your name), this week will be a great week. Things will fall into place as planned. Success is imminent. No matter the situation I will say the right things at the right time to the right people. My words will bring fruit of victory. My thoughts will be more clear and precise leading to the right words. I speak increase and balance in my life. Today, I continue my journey to the top."

# Week 10 Recap and Activity

In what ways have choices you've made changed the course of your life so far?

_____

_____

_____

_____

Why is it important that you learn to say things based on intellect of a situation and not emotion and how will you make the necessary adjustments to do it more moving forward?

_____

_____

_____

_____

Write down one decision that you can make today that can change the outcome of your future.

_____

_____

_____

# Week 11: _____

One thing that I pride myself on is the ability to know when I mentally need to be uplifted or take a break. A lot of times we ignore the signs of mental instability and try to push on. I truly believe that the first step to mental stability is speaking out loud for great mental well-being. Remember, we are products of the words we speak so why not set the tone for good mental health.

"Good morning king/queen. I have complete mental clarity. My mind is strong and at peace. I am not at war with myself. I choose mental freedom. I am free. My thoughts are not my enemy. I am in absolute control of my thinking. I will not allow anything to cause me mental instability. I know when to retreat somewhere quiet so that my mind can relax. I have a respectful, loyal relationship with my mind."

# Week 11 Recap and Activity

Why is mental clarity important to you?

_____

_____

_____

_____

What steps will you take to protect your mental health?

_____

_____

_____

_____

If you could replay a memory that makes you smile all day long over and over, what would it be? Why does this make you smile?

_____

_____

_____

_____

_____

# Week 12: _____

I do not believe there is a such thing as a 'weak' person. True strength is not defined in the ability to pick up heavy objects. Real, God-giving strength is mental and should be defined as the ability to see yourself through any and every obstacle in life. Life is going to happen. You can't control that, but what you can control is your ability to mentally muscle pass the distractions.

"(Say your name), you are more than equipped to win big today! Nothing can shake me. No one can control my thoughts or the narrative for my life except. If I say move, the mountain will shift. If I say go, the angels will fly. Whatever I decide mentally will be done, period. I am the main attraction. I am an example of strength. I will NOT be moved from my path. Today is mine for the taking."

# Week 12 Recap and Activity

What are your greatest strengths and attributes?

_____

_____

_____

_____

Moving forward, describe how you will allow your
mental strengths to guide your steps each day.

_____

_____

_____

_____

_____

What does it mean to you to be strong and name one
reason why you fit this category?

_____

_____

_____

_____

_____

# Week 13: _____

      Sometimes when I think about what I want to accomplish, I look at the situation as though it's alive. What do I mean by that? I treat my goal as something that can hear me speak. For me, it sometimes gets bigger than saying it to myself so I occasionally direct my words to the task or goal itself. Never be afraid to speak to the 'dream' directly. Be specific. Call it out by name. Hey, house in Arlington, it's me again, your friend.

"Hey you, (say the name of the goal such as promotion, house, etc), today belongs to us. Soon we will be together. There will be a few who speak against us, but we rebuke them now in the name of Jesus. We belong with each other. I deserve you. I will not stop until we can embrace. I speak to you now with authority and a knowing that what I desire I can have. What I desire is you, (say the goal)!"

# Week 13 Recap and Activity

When you spoke to your dream/desire with authority and conviction, how did it feel?

_____

_____

_____

Knowing that you can speak to your goals, how often will you attempt to do so and what distractions do you think you need to speak against?

_____

_____

_____

_____

How have you committed self-sabotage in the past with your words and how does that change today?

_____

_____

_____

_____

_____

# Week 14: _____

When I was a young kid, I lived next door to my great aunt, Aunt Lucy. That lady could speak life into a brick wall and it would understand the task and move! She was the first person who taught me the simple task of believing in your dreams. She did not understand the concept of defeat! Everything that she wanted to do in life was done and all boxes had been checked. This week, start to simply believe.

"I believe in me and the idea of <u>(say your name)</u> being successful. I believe that every thought and desire I have is attainable. I believe that God created me to prosper. I believe that nothing can stop me unless I give it permission to do so. And I am going to just say it now, but NOTHING has my permission to stop my dreams! I believe that I will grow stronger mentally. Soon will accomplish what I set out to achieve."

# Week 14 Recap and Activity

Write down why you believe you will accomplish your goals and dreams.

_____

_____

_____

What is that desire you want to accomplish and why is it important to you?

_____

_____

_____

_____

Just like Aunt Lucy inspired me, who can you pull from for inspiration and why do you choose them?

_____

_____

_____

_____

_____

_____

# Week 15: _____

There is a lot of truth behind the idea that we are products of what we think about the most. Many times we don't realize how led we are by our thoughts. When you start the day thinking negatively, usually by the end of the day you can say it was a bad day. When you focus on clearer and more positive thoughts, your day is normally a breeze. Let's normalize cleaning our thoughts daily the same way it's important to bathe.

"I see you, <u>(say your name)</u>. I see the thoughts you have for yourself. Today we move only with good thinking. Today will be a great one. I will be encountered by positive people. My smile will influence someone whether I know them or not. My peace will overflow into the atmosphere and connect with all those around me. I will think peaceful thoughts today. My mind is free of pointless clutter and I feel great!"

# Week 15 Recap and Activity

Why is it important for you to move with fresh, positive thoughts from here on out?

_____

_____

_____

_____

What are some of the most positive thoughts you found yourself experiencing this week?

_____

_____

_____

_____

What exercises will you try in effort to increase your ability to think more positively?

_____

_____

_____

_____

_____

# Week 16: _____

      After my divorce, one of the hardest challenges I faced was learning to love myself again. It was a task. I didn't see life as that important anymore because everything that I thought I was invested in failed. Truth is, loving yourself should come before anything else. It is a non-stop operation no matter the situation. Even if everything goes left, you should still have your sanity. Before anyone else says how much they love you, be sure to tell yourself. You owe it to you.

"I love me. No, really. I truly love me. I don't care who stays or who goes. It doesn't matter if anyone else believes in me or not. I will always have my best interests at heart. I will work hard to gain success for myself. I will treat myself with kindness and respect. I will take care of myself mentally. And I will never allow anyone to make me second guess my worth. I love myself and that's final."

# Week 16 Recap and Activity

Why do you believe it's so important to hear yourself speak love about yourself?

_____

_____

_____

_____

What do you love most about yourself and why?

_____

_____

_____

_____

In a few words, what does a happy day to yourself look like?

_____

_____

_____

_____

_____

_____

# Week 17: _____

When you consider who God is and how wonderfully designed the planet is, you can't help but know that He is the same God that created you. If nature can be so beautifully crafted and built, how much more energy and effort do you think went into your design? This week, if you don't remember nothing else, remember that you are one of God's designs.

"Good morning <u>(say your name)</u>. I am great because God, the creator of the universe and everything we know and see made me. I was wonderfully designed with a purpose. I am not here by mistake and God has a plan for me. Though every day will not be great, I am still a gift to life itself. I am humble. I am amazing. I trust in my abilities and I know that victory is mine to claim. God thank you for making me unique and please bless the steps that I take."

# Week 17 Recap and Activity

How important is it to you that God created you to be great and why?

_____

_____

_____

One of the greatest facts is how there are no two people exactly alike across the board. Some share a lot of similarities but there is always that one thing that makes someone special from everyone else. What makes you different from others, in your opinion?

_____

_____

_____

_____

How does the thought, 'God made me', change your outlook on life?

_____

_____

_____

# Week 18: _____

Doubt and fear has killed more people's dreams than any other force in history. We sometimes get caught up in watching the lives of those around us seeking to compare and contrast without realizing that everyone's path is different. We are ending the idea of limitations from now on. No more creating obstacles for ourselves that didn't exist before. Let's speak demise to limitations!

"There is nothing that can stop me from doing me. I have been equipped with the necessary tools to survive. I am intelligent and creative. I am powerful and tough. I will not create my own barriers. And any barriers that find their way in front of me will be destroyed. I will not allow anything to slow me down. I was created to win and to win big! Today, I focus against all forms of limitations."

# Week 18 Recap and Activity

In what ways have you limited yourself from achieving what you want and how does that change now?

_____

_____

_____

_____

Write down three times you were able to overcome something despite having limitations. What was your mindset each time?

_____

_____

_____

_____

_____

_____

_____

_____

_____

_____

_____

# Week 19: _____

      Taking ownership for the things you want is key. Don't ever be afraid to claim something even if you don't have it yet. Everything was created around you from spoken words. Therefore, we will continue to speak life on what we desire. We will own these things through thought and words until they become a reality. This week let's continue using the power of our voice to call things to be.

      "For a while now I have strongly desired to have (fill in the blank). I believe that this desire will be my reality. I have power in my voice to say what I want and my heart tells me that I can have it. So again, today I speak on having (fill in the blank). I desire to receive this by (give a realistic time frame for this to develop but be specific). I would like to find myself in position to make this yearning come true. Whatever I need to learn or do will be done."

# Week 19 Recap and Activity

What do you desire more than anything in the world
and why is this so important to you?

_____

_____

_____

_____

What are the things you know you need to do in order
to achieve this goal or dream?

_____

_____

_____

_____

How much more convinced are you that this goal is
attainable after speaking on it this week and why do
you feel this way?

_____

_____

_____

_____

# Week 20: _____

There will be times when people will say things about you that could hinder you from working harder to achieve your dreams. Unfortunately, there will be moments when things will be said about you when you are not around. Because words have power, they can still manifest your demise without you even knowing it. An important habit to create is remembering to intentionally speak against the negativity spoken with your name on it.


"I, (say your full name), rebuke any derogatory remarks and comments made about me that are hostile to my success. I am and will continue to be a winner. I will certainly manifest my goal of having (speak your goal by name) and there are no words other than my own that can come against this. It is mine to have and in due time I will achieve it. Today will be an amazing day!"

# Week 20 Recap and Activity

I know firsthand the power of words used against me. Using this activity, write a few things you heard mentioned about you and replace them with something positive. Also, say them out loud after you write them to create a new direction for the words used against you. (ex. I am not weak but I am beyond strong)

_____

_____

_____

_____

_____

_____

Now that we have cancelled the negative words directed towards you, let's end this by saying why you will achieve your goals successfully.

_____

_____

_____

_____

# Week 21: _____

      I can honestly say that I don't believe I would be who I am today if it wasn't for pain. There will be moments in life when things seem to fall apart. It will be as if the world has turned its back on you and you are all alone. There may be times when heartbreak seems to be a normal occurrence. The key is to not allow pain to destroy, but instead use that pain to fuel you. Turn that pain into premium gasoline and make it a point to take charge of what you want. That includes how you want to feel. But it all starts with you.

"Good morning (say your last name). Though times may get rocky and moments can be undesirable, you (point to yourself) were built to win! Your victory will be eternal. Your peace will be everlasting. And pain don't last forever. So TODAY I will focus solely on my victory and my peace. Happiness is mine to gain and I will not settle for less. Be blessed (your name)."

# Week 21 Recap and Activity

I pride myself in knowing what I endured and how I overcame it all to be a better version of me. Take a moment to reflect on one thing, or two if it helps, that you have overcome to remind yourself that you have done it before and can do it again. Be sure to specify what you did to get past that situation.

_____

_____

_____

_____

_____

_____

No matter what happens in life, the greatest thing you can do is love God and love yourself. Name one thing you are willing to do moving forward to remind you that you love YOU.

_____

_____

_____

_____

# Week 22: _____

When I sit back and think about the things that I want to accomplish and the feeling I may have when it happens, nothing feels greater than knowing "why" I want to get it done. When you are tired and ready to tap out, your "why" should push you through. When you begin to believe that you are wasting your time trying, your "why" should change that belief. We will take this moment to reflect on why it's important you cross the finish line.

"Hi (say your name). Today is a beautiful day. In fact, it's a great day. There is no better time than now that I continue to fight for (say your goal). I need to do this because (say why this is so important to you). I will not substitute the importance of my why. I will not back down from achieving my goal because my why depends on it. God, bless me with the strength to fulfill my why! (Say your name), let's conquer the day boss!"

# Week 22 Recap and Activity

In a few words, explain what your "why" is and the reason it is so important to you.

_____

_____

_____

_____

_____

Think back to when your "why" became official for you. Describe the feeling you get when you think about the day you will accomplish your goal and your "why" is fulfilled. How will that feel for you? Explain.

_____

_____

_____

_____

Describe why you can't afford to lose.

_____

_____

_____

# Week 23: _____

      I learned a long time ago that when it's hard to find peace in your life or a particular situation, sometimes you have to be your own peace. You have to find a way to exit the reality you are in by placing your mind and heart somewhere else. This week let's center our focus on creating peace by speaking it into our lives. Peace be with you.

"I, (say your full name), is a recipient of God's perfect peace. Though there may be turmoil or strife around me, my thoughts are with my inner peace. I am calm and serene. My heart is smiling for my future is brighter than my previous days. I will walk by faith and live in abundance. And when I say abundance I do not solely speak of material things. But when I say abundance I speak of joy, happiness, serenity, and tranquility. I am a product of peace."

# Week 23 Recap and Activity

Name one thing in your life that has brought you
peace before. Explain how.

_____

_____

_____

Why is it important for you to feel peace in your life
and what steps do you feel you need to take to
achieve it?

_____

_____

_____

_____

_____

Who are the people in your life that make you feel at
peace? Do they know how you feel about them?

_____

_____

_____

# Week 24: _____

In life, there will be days when it seems that everything you have worked for is going backwards. You will look at the progression meter and it will seem like its stuck. All the effort and energy you are applying towards your goals will start to appear pointless. This, my friend, is where I tell you to trust the process. Whether you are looking to lose weight, buy a home, work towards a degree, or start a business, just to name a few, you may have moments that make you pull your hair. You MUST keep going. The process is not over till it's over.

"Morning (say your name). Today will be a productive day. Things are going my way, even if it doesn't seem like it. This is a vital part of the process. Victory is on the other side. I will not quit. I will not falter. I cannot stop now. Things are going to get greater soon. I appreciate the process. Now let's go win big!"

# Week 24 Recap and Activity

Sometimes, while going through your process, you just need to create a positive outlet to mentally escape the parts of the process that are not easy to absorb. Name some of the things you enjoy to do in your free time that helps you relieve stress and tension. List a couple of days and times you are willing to set aside to focus on these activities weekly while you go through your process.

_____

_____

_____

When you deal with challenging days, the best thing to do is verbally support yourself. Say something uplifting to help you get through. I like to tell myself "Pain don't last forever" when I go through things. Write a sentence that you can use for yourself during those times. Never forget this sentence and USE IT.

_____

_____

_____

# Week 25: _____

       Do you know who your all-time best friend is? What if I told you that they should not be your all-time best friend, but there is one way better than them? You ready for me to tell you who they are? Ok, here you go…you. That's right. You should be your all-time best friend. Not saying you shouldn't have additional best friends but no one can have your back and love on you like you should be able to do yourself. Self-care is the best care and though it takes practice, what do we have to lose? Let's learn to love and treat ourselves better than the expectations we have from others to do so.

"I love you (say your name). I mean it. I really love you and I trust you with all my heart. You support me in ways no one can ever come close. Though I love and recognize those around me who have my back, just know today that I see you as my biggest supporter yet. Be blessed and have a productive day!"

# Week 25 Recap and Activity

Why do you feel it's important that you become your best friend more than anyone else?

_____

_____

_____

I tend to take myself out on dates solo often. It's the most satisfying feeling to treat yourself and become one with yourself. What are a few things that you have never done alone that you would be willing to try once for the experience? (i.e. movies, dinner, amusement park)

_____

_____

_____

What are the qualities you look for in a 'best friend'? Do you meet those qualities for yourself?

_____

_____

_____

# Week 26: _____

Having clear thoughts and laser sharp focus is imperative to growth and success. Many things can happen in life that take away from those elements, but we must find a way to look past the distractions. The reflection/meditation part of the weekly activities is vital because you grow your mental clarity by slowing things down to your speed. At that point, you can dictate the flow and activity level of your thoughts more. This week we will center our focus on speaking to our thoughts.

"Great morning (say your name). Today I will go out with a clear mind and calm thoughts. I will approach life and not wait it to come to me. I am in control of my thoughts. God will guide my steps. Those steps will lead me to success. And my thoughts will not cause me to waver. I am relaxed. I am at peace. I am focused more than I've ever been. Today I move closer to success."

# Week 26 Recap and Activity

Being focused in everything you do allows you a better chance at guaranteeing victory. In what ways has your focus changed in the last 6 months?

_____

_____

_____

_____

_____

Thinking back to when you last got distracted from an important task, what did you do to regain focus to finish the assignment?

_____

_____

_____

What are the activities you will participate in for the next few months to help increase your focus?

_____

_____

_____

# Mid-Year Recap

You have officially finished a half year of affirmations. Round of applause for yourself please. One of the things I hope to do with this project is to create a habit of each individual learning the importance of positive thinking and speaking life on their goals and dreams. We must be intentional with our success in life. Another habit I hope for you to pick up is journaling. The questions that are asked in the recap sections are designed to make you think more about what you want and what you are doing to get there. Most importantly, they are designed to help you take time to write out your thoughts. Although you only do the recap once a week, I would like to challenge you to try it daily even if only 5 minutes a day. So with that being said, before you start next week's affirmation, take a moment to express how you feel from the first half of a year of speaking affirmations each day and explain your expectations for life after making this a habit moving forward. Please take this time to be detailed and open with yourself.

# Week 27: _____

      Many people struggle daily with the simple task of loving themselves. Sounds like it should be a walk in the park to show yourself love but take it from my personal experience, it's harder than you think. I went years battling suicidal thoughts because I did not love who I was. I felt that the world and the people around me would be better off without my presence. That was so far from the truth. Loving yourself is a different gift. If nothing else, we are telling God thank you for life by simply loving ourselves. This week let's remind 'you' how much you love yourself.

"Good morning (beautiful/handsome). I love you. I don't just say that because it sounds good. I truly love you (say your name). The battles we face, we face together. The joys we experience is ours to share. I love myself more than anything else in this world. I thank God for me. Life is great, but so much better with me in it. Be blessed today (your name)."

# Week 27 Recap and Activity

One of the most important things anyone can do in life is love themselves. Not saying be boastful, but genuinely love who they are and what they represent for good. Use this moment to name all the great things you like about yourself from talent to characteristics to just anything you can think of that makes you who you are.

_____

_____

_____

_____

_____

I take pride in making known the people who have influenced me to keep fighting for me. Those that were there to say, "You got this". List the names of the ones who have kept you grounded.

_____

_____

_____

_____

# Week 28: _____

   We live in a world where people are never happy with the skin they're in. I believe the most important part of loving yourself starts with being in love with who you are as you are. Don't worry about the details of how you will lose weight, how you will fix your smile, and other things that don't promote life. The fact of the matter is that you are here, alive and breathing. The things that can be changed safely then do it. But no more stressing over nothing that does not promote LIFE! You are a blessing to a lot of people as you are. God makes no mistakes therefore you have no flaws. You are wonderfully designed.

"Good morning (say your name). I know that I am amazing. I know that God took His time when he made me. I love who I am and who I am becoming. Great things are in store for me and I am more than happy to receive them. I am a gift. I believe that. And today I will continue to live in that truth."

# Week 28 Recap and Activity

I have had people tell me that my smile brings them joy. What is one thing people say that they like about you and what's that one thing you love about yourself?

_____

_____

_____

_____

Many times when we think to change something about us physically it's because we are not at peace internally. Let's break through the inner barrier that is using our appearance as a distraction. What are the things about you that you wish to change internally and name one thing you can do to change it safely.

_____

_____

_____

_____

_____

_____

# Week 29: _____

      The biggest cheerleader in your life should be that person who looks back at you every morning when you brush your teeth. We will all usually have that one person who we can count on to be the loudest in our corner rooting us on, but there should be no one greater cheering for you than yourself. Whether you are saying "YESSS!!" or hyping yourself up in the gym by saying, "This is nothing Rod!", there should be no greater joy than hearing yourself say "You can do it". Let's start back being the premier hype man in our lives.

"What's up boss! Today is another day we will defy the odds and beat the distractions. The biggest challenge today will be (name one challenge), but just like others in the past it will be defeated. I am good and nothing will change that. All I do is win. Failure is not an option! This is my life and I will have everything I set out for. Let's Go (your name)!"

# Week 29 Recap and Activity

Thinking back on the past year, what has been the biggest hurdle you have had to leap and how were you able to conquer it?

_____

_____

_____

Now focusing on the future, what is the ultimate goal for you in life right now, whether career wise or personal like a house or car? What barriers stand in the way and what steps will you take to conquer them?

_____

_____

_____

One last time, let's proclaim victory for yourself by finishing the sentence and saying it out loud. "This year I will accomplish

_____

_____"

# Week 30: _____

      I believe that there is a circle for everyone. Who we allow in our lives is important. Many times the energy we operate from was inherited from the people closest to us. Hence the saying, 'birds of a feather flock together'. It's almost impossible to not adopt the attitude of your best friends and close family members. If you want more in life, spend more time with those doing more. If you want to think bigger, talk to those who speak abundance. How we connect with the right people is done like everything else…we speak it in existence.

"God thank you for this day. I appreciate you for making me amazing. I was created to have more so that I can be a blessing to others. I understand that my circle is important. I have successful people in my life right now. I will meet more of the right people. They will feed me ideas that I never knew. I will grow abundantly with amazing friends."

# Week 30 Recap and Activity

Who are the greatest influencers in your life right now and what makes them special?

_____

_____

_____

_____

_____

In what ways have your friends and closest family helped you elevate in recent years?

_____

_____

_____

_____

What are some steps you feel you need to take to change your circle or is it already where it needs to be?

_____

_____

_____

# Week 31: _____

There is a famous quote used by many successful people that they say when describing their drive to victory. "I was willing to die on the treadmill." This means that no matter how hard it got for them, the option of quitting and letting it go did not exist. Whatever they needed to do or say to themselves to keep pushing is what they relied on. Distractions, obstacles, and the idea of defeat was to be no match. They would have to be carted out first before they stopped striving for success. This week we set the stage that nothing will stop your drive!

"(Your name), you are the master of your fate. No matter what anyone says about me or tries to do to me, I will not lose! I will rise above the clouds. I will fight until the end. My time is now. My moment is now. Failure is only tuition. I will learn from my mistakes and finish strong! Today I take a step closer to greatness. Have an excellent day (your name)."

# Week 31 Recap and Activity

When was the last time you quit something important? What was it and how did it make you feel?

_____

_____

_____

_____

_____

Moving forward, how will you maintain your focus to finish despite what difficulties may take place?

_____

_____

_____

_____

_____

Name 3 reasons why you feel you deserve what you're working towards achieving.

_____

_____

_____

# Week 32: _____

When you practice manifestation, one of the most essential actions to exercise is hearing yourself speak the reward over and over. It's good to see it in your mind. It's great to visualize it while you go on with your day. But one of the things that makes your brain pop is hearing it said continuously. I try not to get too comfortable failing to remember this approach because it can become easy to forget. Make it a legitimate point to say your goal out loud as often as possible.

"Good morning (your name). I see it more clearly than ever. I will have my (say your goal) real soon. I will remain focused and stick to the plan. Having (say your goal) is so visible to me. I feel like I can touch it right now. I was made to achieve this goal. God please lead my steps and create the path necessary for me to obtain (say your goal). Today, I continue my drive for success."

# Week 32 Recap and Activity

Throughout this book, I have been very repetitive on purpose. My goal is to get you to keep focusing on the goal at hand. So again, please list what you desire to achieve and how soon would you like to see this thing manifest itself?

_____

_____

_____

What is the reason you want this goal to be accomplished so badly?

_____

_____

_____

Thinking about your strategy for success, what is one area you need to improve more to get closer to your goal?

_____

_____

_____

# Week 33: _____

       Determining one's purpose in life is one of the most frequently visited topics for individuals as we grow older. Wondering if we are truly fulfilling God's intentions for creating us. What if your true purpose was simply a 'positive word away'? What if whatever we say we are was God's planned purpose for our life? Think about it. If what we say over and over, backed by the belief that we can accomplish it is all it takes to bring things into reality, who's not to say that is where our true purpose lies? Search your heart, seek what fills you with joy, and attack your plan with words to achieve it.

"Good morning (sir/ma'am). I was designed to (say what you desire to do). My age does not matter as today is all that counts. Today I desire to fulfill my ambitions to (speak it again). Only I can stop this from happening. I refuse to get in my own way. Today, I will step into my purpose. I will not stop until it's done."

# Week 33 Recap and Activity

Thinking back to your childhood, what has always been that "thing" that has moved your heart that you really wanted to do and is that still the case today?

_____

_____

_____

_____

Would you say that you are or are not walking in your purpose today and what's the reason for your response?

_____

_____

_____

_____

What motivates you more than anything in life to be successful and why is that so important to you?

_____

_____

_____

# Week 34: _____

When we say positive things to ourselves, it sets a tone that we sometimes don't even realize is taking place. We become a little more immune to negativity that we may face in our day. I have also noticed the attraction of more positive events and news coming my way more often when I start my day with positive speaking. This week we will take it back to the basics and just reignite the light that is already inside of us to start our days.

"Hi (say your name). Today is a great day. The fact that I am in it makes today even better. I am a difference maker. I see my obstacles yet I see my goals and the only thing I'm focused on is achieving my dreams. Nothing will prevent me from being great. I was created by God for this occasion. Life is amazing. I love it and I live to be happy. Peace is my best friend. My mind is at ease. I feel good, therefore I am good. Let's make today count."

# Week 34 Recap and Activity

What do you love about yourself more than anything?

_____

_____

_____

If you could choose to bring peace and joy to anyone in your life today, who would it be and why?

_____

_____

_____

_____

Some days will bring rain and it's hard to stay focused on positivity. What is something that you can do moving forward to offset the potential energy shift to remain positive even if the day doesn't make it easy to do?

_____

_____

_____

_____

# Week 35: _____

Throughout my life, I have had a fair share of individuals that made it their responsibility that I was ok. Whether it meant I was able to get food or making sure I got help with a financial obligation that I was not prepared to handle alone. These people never allowed me to fall. Even when I wanted to curl up and cease to exist, they provided me with resuscitation of life. This week I will speak life into those individuals. We know that words are power even for those we speak on privately. Each day you can say a different name of a friend or family member if you choose.

"Good morning. I am blessed today. Even more so because of people who have made it possible for me to grow. I'd like to bless (say a name) with positive vibes today. May (he/she) have an abundance of peace on today. May their heart be filled with God's unfailing love. The world is a better place because of her/him. Blessings to them always."

# Week 35 Recap and Activity

Who are the top people that have been the safety nets in your life?

_____

_____

_____

_____

What have been some challenges you faced in life and who has been the most available to prevent you from going under? How did they assist you?

_____

_____

_____

_____

Now, let's turn the table slightly. Who have you been a safety net for and in what ways have you been a blessing to them?

_____

_____

_____

# Week 36: _____

      I have a saying I like to use when talking about imagination. If I'm talking with someone about the power of the mind, they may hear me say that every building or structure we see standing before us was built three times before becoming reality. First, someone has to think it. Secondly, those thoughts become blueprints. Simply thoughts of a design on paper. Lastly, that bad boy is built for all eyes to see. But do not lose sight that what we see started in someone's mind first. How powerful is that? Now let me ask this question. What are you thinking? Make it positive and create a verbal blueprint.

"What a beautiful day I have before me. My thoughts are the fruit to my future. My future looks ripe. I will continue to grow spiritually, financially, and healthier. I can and will build everything my heart desires for my complete well-being. My vibe is great. My focus is strong. I am ready to attack the day."

# Week 36 Recap and Activity

What are the visions you have for your future?
Explain in detail please.

_____

_____

_____

_____

_____

_____

_____

How will you take what's in your mind and place it on
a blueprint? Considering a blueprint is a layout of
steps and instructions set in place to build a design,
what does it look like on paper for your dreams to
come to life?

_____

_____

_____

_____

_____

_____

# Week 37: _____

At times when I start my day, I don't necessarily focus on a particular task or goal. In these moments I just want to remind myself of all the great, powerful words that define who I am. Hearing them seems to ignite something inside of me. It's not that I don't believe these words define me beforehand, but once again, there is death and life in the power of the tongue. So I decisively choose life so that nothing can come along and freely take up residence inside my peace of mind. Let's speak life on our life.

"My name is _____ and I am a winner. I lead by example. I trust the process. I am great. I am strong. I am the definition of courageous. I am a product of love. I am intelligent. I am amazingly creative. I am talented and driven. I am a child of God. I was created to succeed. I am a difference maker. I will gain everything that I fight for. I will have a productive day."

# Week 37 Recap and Activity

When you really think about words that define you, what are the top 3 words that stand out and why?

_____

_____

_____

_____

What are 2 words that you know you need to replace in your vocabulary and what will their replacements be?

_____

_____

_____

In your words, why do you think is it important to remember to speak positive words over your life as often as possible?

_____

_____

_____

_____

# Week 38: _____

The definition of trust as it is defined in Google says, "firm belief in the reliability, truth, ability, or strength of someone or something." These are some pretty bold words used in the definition. When you think about these words for a second, which ones define you? Most importantly, in reference to you towards yourself, which of these words relate to how well you trust yourself? If we can't trust anyone else, we must always find a way to prove to ourselves that we will have our own best interests in life. Let's focus on speaking words of power and trust on ourselves.

"Good morning (say your name). I believe in me. I have my best interests at heart. I will not fail myself and continue to fight through all of life's obstacles. I trust my heart. I trust my abilities. I trust that God has secured a spot for me in the realm of success. I will me up and not let myself down. Right now is my season of victory."

# Week 38 Recap and Activity

What attributes do you trust most about yourself?

_____

_____

_____

In what ways have you already fulfilled your promise
to yourself in life?

_____

_____

_____

_____

Who did you trust most in your life and how did they
help you get to where you are today?

_____

_____

_____

_____

Finish this sentence. "I trust that I will

_____
                                                                  "
_____

# Week 39: _____

     I feel that life has become such a task of making great impressions for social media and trying to bestow a certain image, that we have forgotten how to live in the moment and have fun. Yes, it's important that we focus on goals and plans. I agree that we must be serious about life and what it has to offer. But I also truly believe that enjoyment of life surpasses everything. Let's be children again. Let's see life from a lens that all opportunities are possible and fun to reach.

"This is an amazing morning and this will be an incredible day, (say your name). So many opportunities will be available for me to grow. Life is good. I am enjoying every aspect of it. I will live abundantly and I will be in control of my peace. My days are bright and excitement will be the music of my heart. My smiles will open doors therefore I will love to smile. Everything is working for in my favor."

# Week 39 Recap and Activity

What is the most exciting memory you have as a child?

_____

_____

_____

_____

_____

What is the best memory you have as an adult?

_____

_____

_____

_____

In your imagination, what will celebrating a successful moment for you look like?

_____

_____

_____

_____

_____

# Week 40: _____

      I'm not sure what you believe, but I wholeheartedly think that God's grace is more than enough to get me where I need to be in life. But just like anything else that I could use to help propel myself to the next level, I have to trust God's grace in my life. How do you begin to trust that? By proclaiming it. Using your voice to announce to yourself and whoever can hear you that you take ownership as a recipient of God's grace in your life. Today, we start creating the habit of accepting His grace and mercy for the direction of our lives.

"I, (state full name), am a suitable recipient for God's grace. I will be led by my heart to trust God and all that He has instilled in me. I know that no weapon formed against shall prosper. I believe that God's grace is sufficient for me to survive and thrive. I am here by the power granted to me by the Creator. I will win because that's what I was created to do."

# Week 40 Recap and Activity

In what ways has God set you up to succeed?

_____

_____

_____

_____

_____

There will be many days harder than others. In what
ways have you been able to maintain your faith in the
idea that you will succeed in everything that you
planned to do?

_____

_____

_____

_____

In your words, how do you define God's grace?

_____

_____

_____

_____

# Week 41: _____

    I know you have heard me constantly talk about power in the tongue, but I'm not sure if you realize just yet how strong that statement really is. There are certain groups in Africa that use no medicinal procedures at all when it comes to healing. They literally speak the illness out. Healing is simply a state of mind in most cases. There are several placebo studies where one group was given actual medicine and the other group a pill that wasn't actually medicinal yet both groups healed not knowing who had the real medicine. We will begin the practice of speaking great health to our bodies.

"I love myself. I, (say your name), declare a healthy body healed of all negative entities. I claim peace over my body. I speak wellness over my body. My organs are strong and I feel amazing. Sickness has no place in me. I am healed and whole. I am in my right mind and I engage in positive thinking. I am free."

# Week 41 Recap and Activity

Name a time when you saw words spoken manifest themselves. What was your reaction?

_____

_____

_____

_____

What are some things you feel you should speak against as it pertains to your health? Answer by speaking an affirmation over yourself in that regard.

_____

_____

_____

_____

What would be some challenges that you may have to overcome to increase your belief in this situation?

_____

_____

_____

_____

# Week 42: _____

What has the power to make or break you? Is it what others think of you? Is it what someone says about you? Is it the environment you were raised or currently live? Ask yourself if there is a such force or power available that has authority to make you great or cripple your progression. Can I give you the answer? The force that has all the power in the world to dictate who you are and who you become is looking right back at you in the mirror. That's who you look in the eyes and say loudly and proudly what you will accomplish. And when you do, make sure you mean every single word that is said. You got this.

"I, (say your name), am proud to say that I am victorious. Though the battle is not over, I already claim everything that I'm fighting for. I will (say your goal). Nothing or nobody will stop that. God has given me the authority to succeed. That's what I plan to do. I will accept nothing less than greatness for my life!"

# Week 42 Recap and Activity

Regardless of what anyone has said in the past, who do you say are?

_____

_____

Describe what success will look like for you when it's all said and done.

_____

_____

_____

Give 3 powerful words that currently describe your strengths.

_____

_____

There is always someone watching you waiting for you to fall. But here I want you to focus on who you believe wants to see you win the most and what that person means to you.

_____

_____

# Week 43: _____

Many times, we as individuals look for the light at the end of the tunnel in dark or difficult situations. It is during these times that I suggest you dig deep to be the very light that you are looking for. I believe that each of us has been given enough light within to overcome all obstacles and turbulence that life may bring. Don't look for the light any longer. The light is you. You are the end of the dark tunnel. You are the one shining bright enough that others can see and follow. How do you access this internal light you ask? By claiming it.

"I, (say your name), am the light that everyone is looking for. I am the light that shines bright throughout all dark situations. I am the one creating the flow and not simply following the wave. I follow God's guidance which has gifted me with the ability to help others and myself. I believe in me. I will continue to shine."

# Week 43 Recap and Activity

What do you feel is your greatest strength and why do believe so?

_____

_____

_____

_____

What is your shining moment in life? Describe a moment in time when the odds were stacked against you and somehow you found a way out. How did that make you feel?

_____

_____

_____

_____

Who have you been the 'light at the end of the tunnel' for in your life? Why is this person so important to you?

_____

_____

# Week 44: _____

When I was very young, older people would always make us focus on what we wanted to be when we grew up. It was always about the career path and where we'd make a living. I believe the most important thing to prepare us on was how often we would face failure and loss in the future. We should understand early that failure isn't the end result. No matter if it is business or losing a loved one, learning how to deal with those matters head on when they hit requires preparation. Part of the way that we prepare is by speaking life over the future hurt feelings. Allow your mind to find a place to rest in the event of failure.

"Good morning (king/queen). I know that there may be difficult days ahead. I understand that life won't always be easy. I also understand that I am strong and my mind is powerful. I can withstand any pain that comes my way. I will lean on to God's perfect peace in moments of chaos. I will overcome all odds."

# Week 44 Recap and Activity

What was a defining moment in your life when things seemed to hit the fan?

_____

_____

_____

What do you feel has been the best way for you to overcome obstacles when they present themselves?

_____

_____

_____

_____

_____

In what way do you feel you were prepared early on to handle bad outcomes and situations in your life and are those preparations still valid for you today?

_____

_____

_____

_____

# Week 45: _____

     Everything around us seems so different than one decade ago. One thing I remember from a while back is talking with a group about how people fear change. The older generations from my youth never wanted things to change. I occasionally still see elderly people write checks at the grocery store instead of using debit cards. I believe that change is great in all facets. In order to grow, change is inevitable. You cannot accept a higher level in any aspect of life with the same mindset as the level before. Change has to take place. This week we will invite change into our minds. We will prepare our hearts to embrace the new things that will occur.

"I gladly accept positive change into my life. I have to escape from my current cocoon in order to grow. I will increase spiritually, financially, and mentally. Change will not hinder me. It will be my elevator to the next level. My day will be great."

# Week 45 Recap and Activity

What changes have taken place in your life that have benefited you positively? Did you originally accept these changes in a positive manner or did they have to grow on you?

_____

_____

_____

_____

What changes do you feel need to take place for you to achieve your future goal/dream?

_____

_____

_____

_____

In what ways are you prepared to accept new changes in your life moving forward in order to experience increase?

_____

_____

# Week 46: _____

    A smile is such a powerful force. There are times when a simple smile could alter a complete stranger's day. You may feel that the world is cruel and nothing good can come from it and then BOOM…you see a beautiful smile and it's changes your entire thought process. You are probably the one who rendered the smile that reversed suicidal thoughts in someone without knowing it. Never underestimate the power of a warm, heartfelt smile. It could be the very reason someone's day becomes brighter. So if you don't do anything else this week, smile.

"This will be a great day, (say your name). I am happy. I have complete peace. My life has a purpose. My smile is my weapon against the enemy. Negativity cannot enter. My smile won't allow it. My thoughts are healthy and sharp. My spirit cannot be broken. Today, I will make someone's life better, somehow."

# Week 46 Recap and Activity

Describe a time you witnessed a smile so beautiful that it made you smile. What were your thoughts and how did it change your day after that?

_____

_____

_____

_____

Our greatest weapon is our ability to laugh and love. What are some of the things in your life that remind you to smile, laugh, and love? Why do these things have such an effect on you?

_____

_____

_____

What is your all-time favorite moment in life that still makes you smile? Describe the moment.

_____

_____

_____

# Week 47: _____

There will be instances when you are faced with doubters. There will come a time where one person makes it clear that they don't believe you can accomplish a goal. This is usually detrimental to your thought process and focus. It's difficult to look past certain negativity especially if it comes from someone you love. But we won't focus on them or the action. We will focus on the words that they may use against you because that's where the power lies. We will focus together on destroying words used against you.

"Good morning (say your name). I am a major part of God's plan. No words formed against me shall prosper. I am not the negative words that have been used in opposition to me. I am remarkable. I am dynamic. I am driven. I am successful. I am worth it. My goals will be crushed and my dreams will be reality. I am of a winning design. I will conquer the day!"

# Week 47 Recap and Activity

Let's take a moment once more to focus on those that love you the most. What has been the most motivating thing someone said to you that pushed you to go harder and who said it?

_____

_____

_____

Pick 3 negative words that were used against you and replace them with one word that represents who you are. We are redirecting the narrative of your life and removing the words that do not belong.

_____

_____

_____

When you see the positive results of your future during your reflection time what does it look like?

_____

_____

_____

# Week 48: _____

What is faith? According to Merriam-Webster dictionary, faith is an allegiance to a duty or person. It also states a belief and trust in and loyalty to God. Are you faithful to yourself? Do you trust in God? Would you say that you claim an allegiance to your dreams and goals? The desires you have in life are very attainable. You just have to believe that they are. Never discount the idea that you will accomplish the task at hand. No one will believe in your goal the way you will. Have faith that it is yours and commit your plans to the Lord and watch them succeed.

"Faith is a part of my identity. The very things that my heart desires will become my reality with the help of God. I trust in my ability to learn the necessary skills and information needed to grow in my purpose successfully. My dreams are attainable. My success is inevitable. I have the winning formula which is faith."

# Week 48 Recap and Activity

What do you believe you can accomplish and what makes your belief so strong?

_____

_____

_____

Describe your prayer life and how often you pray. What are your prayers normally centered around?

_____

_____

_____

_____

When I want something bad enough I place a time table on it. My faith tells me that I will get it in or around that time. If you had to place a date on your dreams today, when would you like to see it come to fruition and are you willing to stand on that date in faith?

_____

_____

# Week 49: _____

      When you stop to think about how massive and great a mountain is, it's hard not to wonder how in the world they were created. Better yet, when thinking about the power, depth, and size of an ocean I become flabbergasted about how such a marvelous thing was formed. It's safe to say that God is amazing simply from these two aspects alone which brings me to a phenomenal point. If the same God that created mountains and oceans created you, how powerful are you? Just like nature is a force to be reckoned with so are you. Now it's time to remind yourself of the authority and power God gave you.

"(Say your name), you are powerful. There is absolutely nothing that I cannot do. I have the strength of an ocean. The fierceness of a storm. I will finish everything that I started with precision. My steps have been guided to greatness. Success is my byproduct. I am a force in this world. Today will be a great day."

# Week 49 Recap and Activity

Describe how confident you feel reciting this week's affirmations. Explain the reason for your answer.

_____

_____

_____

_____

Explain where you believe you gain your power to overcome the difficult challenges you've had to face in life.

_____

_____

_____

_____

How has life prepared you to be stronger as you grow older and more determined to accomplish your goals?

_____

_____

_____

_____

# Week 50: _____

      My life has had a great deal of ups and downs. There have been days where I checked out mentally. Many of the situations I have experienced could have caused major health concerns and even worse. I could have allowed these moments to defeat me and drag me under water. Then I began to do something different. I started to search for the good in all the bad. Believe it or not there is always something good in every bad situation. Some are harder to find than others but the key is expanding your focus on one thing, either the good or the bad. Why not choose the good? Let's work together to find the good in everything.

"I will not focus on the negative. I will see the goodness in everything. I will use each situation to grow mentally. I will not alter my stance during difficult moments. I am a victor. I am unbothered. Only positive vibes may enter my spirit. Today will be phenomenal."

# Week 50 Recap and Activity

What is the worse situation that you have had to face
in your life? Now, take a moment to really think about
what happened in that moment. What's one good
thing you can take from that experience that could
help you grow?

_____

_____

_____

_____

_____

In order to maintain a positive outlook on life
sometimes it requires you to reposition the
relationships in your life. Without calling names, what
are some ways you can separate yourself from
negative people in your circle?

_____

_____

_____

_____

_____

# Week 51: _____

      Life is a beautiful thing. I really appreciate the life I have now. Through all the rain and storms that life may bring, I am still here and stronger than ever before. I believe that is your story too. I know that you have experienced some bad days. Some moments that made you question your decisions and friendships. There may have been times that you didn't think you would make it. But guess what? You made it. You are right here right now and things are only going up from here. Keep loving yourself and confessing that love consistently. You got this boss!

      "Life has been beyond great for (say your name). I am focused on becoming a better me today than I was yesterday. There is nothing more beautiful than life. I will be a spark in someone's life simply because they will see how much I love me. My heart is happy. My spirit has peace. My day will be amazing."

# Week 51 Recap and Activity

Name a time in your life that you would replay over if you had a time machine and explain what made this moment so great.

_____

_____

_____

_____

_____

What brings you complete happiness above everything in life and why?

_____

_____

_____

_____

If you could do one thing in this world to bring joy to the masses, what would it be?

_____

_____

_____

# Week 52: _____

This has been a fun experience. I hope that you have enjoyed this as much as I have. I have spent years off and on starting my mornings with positive affirmations. I have noticed that most of the things that I said during those days presented themselves after a couple of days of consistent reciting. We are products of the things we say. We must continue to focus on saying the positive things and allowing them time to manifest. The key is staying consistent, having faith, and making it fun. We are destined for greatness and will see the top if we don't lose sight. I'll see you there.

"I am destined for greatness. Life will get better each day. I am a positive influence and I attract positive people. I will continue to learn from my mistakes and produce a more fruitful life. My days will see more peace. My mind is free from clutter. I'm a movement that produces winning. Today will be productive."

# Week 52 Recap and Activity

How much have you enjoyed performing the morning affirmations and will you commit to continuing this as a lifestyle change?

_____

_____

_____

_____

What changes have you noticed in your life after doing the morning affirmations for one year?

_____

_____

_____

How much more confident are you now than you were a year ago on reaching your goals? Explain in detail why you feel that way.

_____

_____

_____

_____

# Your Thoughts in a Flash

_____

_____

_____

_____

_____

_____

_____

_____

_____

_____

_____

_____

_____

_____

_____

_____

_____

_____

_____

# About the Author

Rod Shipp is a native of Memphis, TN and grew up in the Binghampton community. He attended the University of Tennessee at Martin where he earned a Bachelor of Science in Sports Management that he used to work as a personal trainer for a number of years. He wrote his first book in college titled, "My Loud Silence", which was a compilation of poetry he had written dating back to his middle school days. He never published the book, but realized at this moment that this was a passion he wanted to pursue.

His first published work was "Rain From a Cloudless Sky" which is available on www.lulu.com along with his motivational book titled "Current Mood: Staying Ready to Succeed". He has more work coming soon as well as a desire to release plays in the near future.

Today, Rod is a successful business owner and entrepreneur and has his sights set on becoming a fulltime investor over the course of the next 5 years or sooner. He loves giving back to those who are less fortunate and spends a great deal of time encouraging and motivating those around him to strive higher and fight harder to achieve their dreams. In short, he is an amazing human being who is ready to take on the world to achieve more. Be sure to follow him on Facebook @RodShipp and Instagram @Rod.Shipp and get the latest on all his latest work and activities. Peace and Blessings.

# Acknowledgements

This has been a fantastic year so far. I am extremely grateful for all my friends and family. My fans and supporters are more than amazing and I am excited to be able to live my dream. I won't stop until I make it where I want to be. I am going to see 'Best Selling Author' status one day. I will speak this in existence. I want to go on record first and thank God for the gift He has given me that has allowed me the joy to write and share my thoughts with the world. Without Him I am nothing! I also would like to thank my team Venisha Brooks, Tequilla Calhoun, Jada Cox, Tamika Williams, and Astria Colbert for helping me make the book signings effortless as well as my editor Tara Schukert for her guidance in keeping things in order with the text. I would like to thank my fellas Steven "Polo" McRae, Howard Branch, Jeff Higgins II, Dr. Nolyn Johnson Jr., David Jordan, Jr., and Galen Jones. My church family at Greater Pleasant Hill Missionary Baptist Church in Memphis and my pastor/brother in law Corey Alexander and my sister LaQuisa Alexander. My aunts Shema, Tolly, and Jackie Thomas. My brother Courtney and sisters Allyson and Kandy. My mom Tammy Bowles and friends Pam Robinson and Jonathan Pierce. I love y'all and there is nothing you can do about it! Stay tuned and ready because there is plenty more to come! Peace and Blessings…Peace!

Peace and Blessings…Shipp